Meditations on the Mysteries of the Holy Rosary

Patrick McGuire

PublishAmerica
Baltimore

Softcover 9781462664313
PUBLISHED BY PUBLISHAMERICA, LLLP
www.publishamerica.com
Baltimore

Printed in the United States of America

Meditations on the Mysteries of the Holy Rosary

by Patrick McGuire

And I who am here dissembled
Proffer my deeds to oblivion and my love
To the posterity of the desert and the fruit of the gourd.

-T.S. Eliot, "Ash Wednesday"

Seventh Sun
Books
2012

In memoriam

Rose McNally McGuire,

Who died on the Feast of the

Immaculate Conception,

2006

Foreword

At my mother's funeral, my brother Johnny, a deacon of the Roman Catholic Church, gave a lovely homily. Much of its goodness came from the subject of Johnny's discourse: our mother and her faith, and especially her devotion to the Holy Rosary. On the night my mother died, I had reminisced with my children about her and my dad and the wonderful gifts they had given me and their other children. From our father, all of us received a certain charm, a generous smile, a happy respect for le mot juste, the ability to laugh as well as to dispute, and so much more. My mother's gifts were as a multifaceted as those from Dad, but two—at least to me— seemed to stand out above the rest. Whatever in me is gentle comes from her. In me, however, gentleness may merely be a splash; in her, it was a wide and deep reservoir. The other important gift that she gave is the Holy Rosary. The statue of the Blessed Mother that stood on her bedroom dresser for fifty years (that I know of) is a symbol of Mary's place in my mother's life. So brother Johnny's homily resonated through me as he spoke that day and for long afterwards. He made me want to acknowledge, in some special way, my gratitude to her for the Gift of Beads. And I call it the Gift of Beads even though, when I say the Rosary, I don't use beads; I count the decades, like a little boy, on my fingers.

When my sisters, collecting and distributing Mom's meager final possessions, sent me the pamphlet that she had used to meditate upon mysteries of the Rosary, I saw my chance. My mother always encouraged me in my literary pursuits; as an avid knitter of sweaters and afghans, she loved yarn, she knew I loved yarns. (Another gift from Dad: the Gift of Yarns!) She may not have always understood what I was up to, literarily, but she was for it, decidedly. When my first (paying) publication came out, for example, Mom cut it from the newspaper, matted it, and presented me with a framed copy. That encouragement, I discovered in re-reading her Rosary pamphlet, has never left me. I suddenly felt that I could acknowledge the Gift of Beads by trying to put in words, in homage to her, what I know and learn and re-learn and feel when I think about the mysteries of the Rosary.

Hence these meditations.

But a quick caveat. My mother's Rosary, as far as I know, remained uninfluenced by what may come to be thought of as John Paul II's most important encyclical. In Rosarium Virginis Mariae, the Pontiff proposed five additions to the Rosary, what he called The Mysteries of Light. My poetic sequence includes these Luminous Mysteries.

-Patrick McGuire

The Joyful Mysteries

I. The Annunciation

A sudden blow of wind, bright angled light
as at Earth's first awakening from night,
a voice unworldly, unembodied, unwarm.

She hears: "Blessed woman, I do no harm,
Mary, sole mother of God and whole,
replete with grace, holy, and pure of soul."

Later, when the night has come, and the flame
of a candle steadies, all seems the same
except, in her veins, the angel's message pounds.

Is this the joy of Yahweh that abounds?
Pregnant? She who's known no man is with child?
Was ever a girl's fantasy more wild?

Asleep. Dreaming her very Joseph's angelic dream:
She rises, married, to God's corporeal scheme.

II. The Visitation

Three days' walking: fleeing a small town's shame?
Nausea in the morning. The belly roiled,
Gone big now, unavoidably obvious.

Three days' wait, and then Elizabeth's claim:
Nausea in the morning; old age foiled,
And a sterile womb grown copious.

Then: "Mary, above all, you are blessed in name
And the fruit is blessed for which you have toiled
And yours is as is mine: Miraculous!"

Fertile fetus kicks within that old dame;
It greets the embryonic Anointed.
And Mary answers in words measured and marvelous.

My soul proclaims, my spirit rejoices:
The Lord hath made large His small handmaiden.
I join the choir of heavenly voices.

I'm given the best of all God's choices:
To carry the child of God's creating.
My soul proclaims, my spirit rejoices.

"A splendid gift Eve could not enjoy," says
the Lord, "for you, O Daughter, is laden.
You join the choir of heavenly voices.

"You are the pure lady I employ," says
the Lord, "to squash the snake-head of Satan."
My soul proclaims, my spirit rejoices.

My child comes, Earthly words to destroy, says
My soul, and the sad world's hollow prating.
We join the choir of Heavenly voices.

I'm given the best of all God's choices:
To magnify the Lord with this stating:
My soul proclaims, my spirit rejoices.
I join the choir of Heavenly voices.

III. The Nativity

♫♫ Haste! Haste to bring Him laud,
the Babe, the Son of Mary. ♫♫

Common odor of dung,
Spit dripped from a cow's tongue,
A sheepdog's sour territorial mark,
Ovine bleatings and brays
Of donkeys, a gray haze
So thick a candle becomes a mere spark,
And dark fluttering barn sparrows,
A cloth bucket, a manger, and two wheelbarrows:

To this place Mary comes,
Apart from inns and homes
Been told "no rooms available tonight."
A kindly woman leads,
points the way. Joseph heeds,
walks softly through streets uneven and tight
and seeks that for which he inquired:
shelter for her who'd said, "Oh, Joseph, I'm so tired."

They are led to a barn
On the outskirts of town.
Worn-out, decrepit and utterly poor—
It stands weak, wind-blown,
Tottering, a thing alone
but for cattle that greet them at the door.
The woman stays, draws the water,
Fluffs the straw, shoos the man and calls Mary daughter.

Mary's lower back aches
And her large belly quakes.
Water leaks from between her legs; the spasms start.
Breath is short; voice is dumb;
wearied limbs now seem numb.
She sighs in pain to calm her pounding heart.
Supine in the straw, strength near-spent,
Skirt-upped, wide-thighed, the Virgin feels the Babe's descent.

Like most infants, It crowns
then holds back. Mary's sounds
are wordless moans, inarticulate grunts
that the woman answers
squeezing her hands with *hers*—
to no avail, for nothing that pain blunts—
while Mary thrusts with meager strength,
the Babe's shoulders come ripping through, then His full
length.

At dawn, shepherds arrive
Like lost bees to a hive,
Mary as queen, and they bring not nectars
But hard bread and goat cheese,
Sour wine, their gifts to please
parents of the Child spoke of by strangers,
poor parents of a new-born king
told by strangers, who had invited them to sing.

Song now becomes anthem.
The strangers sing with them
In harmonies before this day unheard

Lifting the shepherds' voice
To lofty height's rejoice
Where *kingly*, *majestic*, *lord* are one word:
Immanuel, God is with us—
God em-bodied, born in a barn. Miraculous!

♫♫ Haste! Haste to bring Him laud,
the Babe, the Son of Mary. ♫♫

IV. The Purification

Leviticus stipulates: a male child
is impure from the womb and must await
seven days before his circumcision
may be allowed; the mother, thereafter,
must wait thirty-three days of impurity
before she may join her husband and son
in synagogue.
               On the fortieth day,
Mary entered shyly and full of promise,
observance would make her pure and bind
her again to family. An old blind man
became animated; an old woman
beside him, her eyes abrim with tribute,
rose and reached the table of turtle doves
as Joseph paid a tuppence to the changer,
who begrudgingly gave them the two birds
and snorted at their country bashfulness.
The old woman drew close, touched Mary's sleeve
and spoke: "You are she whom I've awaited,
blessed woman, and this the blessed Child."

Then Mary, in accord with tradition,
offered sacrifice while Joseph observed
and Anna, the old woman, elated,
brought forward Simeon, the blind old man,
who had hoped a lifetime for this moment,
who had awaited all his life this moment.

"Mother," he said, "I know not who you are

but this Child I know, for great is the Lord
who made this Child, great and everlasting
are your joys, and great shall be your sorrow:
a *pilum* shall pierce your heart for this Child
and peace will seem to have perished until,
as the Psalm says, Joy cometh in the morning—
Now I may die, for God keeps His promise."

When Mary walked beside Joseph holding
the Child, she grew sad and frightened because,
what had seemed clear, so angelically clear,
yesterday and days before, now wasn't,
now wasn't, now wasn't clear at all.

V. The Discovery

i

The son of a shepherd herds lambs
the son of a baker kneads dough
the son of a wine merchant stomps grapes
the son of a carpenter pounds nails
So what's this? The Child teaching the elders of law?

They had turned from the journey home
The seder, all been said
The Passover, over
The parties, departed.

They had turned from the journey home
only to discover the Child as pedagogue,
not lost nor dead, His voice echoing in the synagogue

They stand without understanding
Rapt in wonderment, their minds wandering in rapture

ii

Summoned from such solemn talk,
the Child obediently bids farewell

and races boyishly to those who raised Him
to mirror their request with His questioning look.
But no, their words go forward first:

The seder had all been said
Passover was over
Our party had departed
Along the road we rode

Men with men, women with children
Or walked if talk was good.
But not you in any shape or hue. Why?
To take my father's business farther.
Did you not know? No.

The Luminous Mysteries

I. The Baptism

John excoriates the excesses of his fellow Jews
offers them two paths to choose:
continue lives of blasphemous lust and greed
or pause here beside the common reed.

Baptism, as John so explains,
washes away the unquiet soul's aches and sprains
and gives seekers a new start
fortified with changes in are pentent heart.

And so for John's words they pause in numbers curious.
Blind ears are ruinous
for those too envious, too furious, too cowed,
insatiable or proud.

And John, so he states, is not
Elijah, nor the Chosen One, nor the prophet,
but a messenger screaming
near the dunes,the Kingdom of God is teeming.

Looking for His cousin, the Man comes riverside
and then wades into the tide;
John says, It is You who should be baptizing me
for it's I who's unworthy.

Let us do all that is right
in custom and in law, in this day's white, bright light.

And so the Man is immersed
in the Jordan waters and from the sky outbursts

a pigeon, which hovers whitely above the two,
speaks when ablutions are through:
This is my Son and upon Him my favors rest.
The Man goes to shore, gets dressed

And out into the desert walks alone.

II. The Wine

i

At a wedding in Cana,
Mary sits beside the Man and His friends.
They are drinking wine,
dipping bread into the center bowls of oils and sauces and
honey.
eating meats and yams and lentils,
savoring oranges and grapes and figcakes
and drinking wine.

Women with trays carry food and empty plates and spoons.
Men with full leather pouches fill cups with more wine.
Men clap tambours; others pluck the table harp.
Timbrels and cymbals sound.
Dance lines move in waves and circles.
Everyone is drinking wine.

Light, the mere light of the sun, envelopes everyone,
warms the chill breezes that blow from the hills,
makes the shaded wine seem cool.
The host implores his guests:
Drink up, drink up,
for I have married today.
Drink with me, for I am happy.
The Man smiles and Mary smiles:
for the bride is lovely and shy;
the groom, a dark beautiful youth.
Mary smiles and the Man smiles:

for weddings remind everyone of the pure
treasures of life, the sure
pleasures of life: sweetness and light.
And everyone is drinking wine.

ii

Mary pulls the sleeve of the Man,
who turns from conversation
to ask what she needs.
For herself, she needs nothing.
"But the host needs something. The wine has run out."
Woman, says the Man, *how does your worry concern me?*
My time has not yet come.
But Mary signals to one of the men with the leather pouches.
"This is my son. Listen to Him."
The Man tells him to fill the ceremonial jars
with water, all six with water.
Then take a sample to the headwaiter.
--who tastes and is astounded.
"Strange," he says. "Most hosts serve first their better wine.
But this wine!"

And when the men with leather pouches
begin again to fill the cups of those singing,
Mary pulls His sleeve again and smiles when He again turns
to her.
She thanks Him and sees in His eyes a new seriousness
as if the pleasures and treasures
of life were no longer sure or pure,
for, she realizes, He has just uncloaked Himself
with this small miracle for her; has come out of hiding.

Anyone who thinks cannot avoid
surmising what He has done;
Anyone who walks in the dark cannot avoid
the light on a hill.Anyone who drinks this wine
will know.
And everyone is drinking.

III. The Sermon

🎵🎵 We are the Light of the World 🎵🎵

They come. Multitudes.
Sweating in the heat.Carrying their sick.
Needing food. Hungering for something they cannot say.
Holding the hands of their young. Guiding their blind
neighbors.
They are frightened, joyful, awed, dubious, sarcastic, hopeful.
The curious come from far away, having walked for days.
A group of lepers, standing apart, awaits him. Prostitutes
and soldiers, taxmen and highwaymen, students and teachers.
Men and women with crutches and slings, odorous
and unwashed; women and men with strange lumps,
odd discolorations, scars and bruises, and toothless grins.
They all wait. The disciples, the synagogue priests,
the widows. Farmers want to see what grows
from His words. Builders wait to know how straight
His plan. Mothers wish to decide how steady
His hand. Vintners wonder how sweet
His fruits, and bakers seek a sample of His
teaching.
The air is still. The sky, cloudless.

The Man speaks to them:
Blessed are they who are low; they shall be raised to heaven.
Blessed are they who are empty; they shall be filled in heaven.
Blessed are they who weep; they shall laugh.

A breeze from the plain behind them cools them

but the clear light of the sun blinds them
as it shines behind Him into their faces.

The Man speaks to them:
*Blessed are the merciful, for they shall be forgiven by the
Father.*
*Blessed are the peacemakers, for they shall be loved of their
Father.*
*Blessed are the hated, the insulted, and the persecuted for my
sake.*
their reward shall be great in heaven.

The breeze continues, and the sun, growing more golden,
lights the faces of those who watch Him.

The Man speaks to them:
But woe to the rich,
and woe to the sated,
*and woe to the blithely indifferent, for they have had their
reward.*

Then He tells them to sit: hundreds, thousands maybe.
And He tells them to remain calm.
His closest followers He calls to Him,
tells them He will feed these multitudes now and here.

♫♫ We are the Light of the World ♫♫

IV. The Transfiguration

Mount Tabor, east of Nazareth, rises
gently to a shelf where goats and sheep graze
and shepherds dwell in limestone cottages.
A morning's sweat of labor is that climb
to those mean abodes, and there one may beg
a cool spot for momentary rest or
shelter from a storm that comes on sudden.
The friendly shepherds offer wine, flatbread
and a small neighborly piece of roasted
mutton to the Man and his followers.
Then the flat terrain meets steep incline
way up to the crest. No footpath to ease
the journey, and few trees to help the hoist.
This part of the ascent takes till evening.
When they reach the top, their legs sore, their breath
no longer theirs, they see beyond the flats
and beyond Tiberias and further
to the Sea of Galilee, where the Man
had stridden on the turbulent waters.
Like Moses on Horeb, like Elijah
on Sinai, He has climbed to talk to God
and has brought His faithful friends Peter, James
and John, who now lie asleep in clover
chilly with falling night and rising wind.

The Man begins to pray. And two others
who were not with Him before suddenly
are there praying, not with Him but to Him.
They are Moses, the man to whom God gave

the Law, and Elijah, the man on whom
God rested the burden of renewing
the covenant of old when His chosen
had gone far, far astray. They glorify
the Man, and He begins to radiate
from within a light: vivid and glowing,
luminous like snow, but warm like the sun,
brilliant like the sun, but visible like
flowering lotem—all radiating
from the Man, shining like daylight, sunlight,
bright light through His translucent skin, more than
a gleam, a glare, a glow: a luminous,
vigorous whiteness, a warm, capacious
brilliance, transformed
into sheer color of sheerness and pure white
of whiteness.
Peter is awake and stands
awed and immobile, and James and John wake.
But Peter sees in the Man's face—which is
white as a leper's skin, but not unclean—
that stern gentleness that first called Peter
to become a fisher of men and now
allows him to approach. "Master," says he,
"we shall build three booths like those of the Feast
of Tabernacles: One for Moses, one
for Elijah, and one for You, Master."
The group is engulfed by a cloud, and a voice
proclaims: *This is my Son. Listen to Him.*

When the cloud goes, Moses and Elijah
are gone. Stars in the sky are visible
once more, and the Man's face is god-pure white

no longer. "O Master," whispers Peter
like a child who has erred, but says no more.
Tell no-one what you have seen till <u>after</u>.
They descend in the cool morning shadows
stopping again for bread, water and wine
at the shepherds' cottages on the green
shelf of Mount Tabor, east of Nazareth.

V. The Feast

On the day before He died, a death freely
accepted, the Man sends some followers
to Temple with the sacrificial lamb,
and He and others prepare the seder.

In an upper room, they draw low couches
around centered tables and set up stacks
of sauce bowls and plates and rows of matzah,
bring in wine and water and bitter herbs.

But the Man kneels before a follower
and begins washing his feet; he protests,
but the Man shushes him and continues
and moves to another and another

until all in the room have had their feet
scrubbed and dried, as Mary Magdalen once
laved His feet, but with her tears, and dried them,
but with her long black hair, soft and clean.

When all are seated, comes the first blessing
and everyone is drinking, and talk turns
round to matzah and symbols of the day
and someone declaims the second blessing

and everyone is singing, and comes then
the food, the sweet and the bitter, and talk
turns round to Egypt, to captivity,
to Exodus and to God Redeemer

as it should have. Thus comes the third blessing:
The meal served, the Man rises with matzah:
Blessed be Thou, Father, and Creator
of the Universe, Who made wheat and grain,
Who made fruits of the vine and Who made work
for human hands, Blessed be Thou, and you
my brothers and my sisters, take this bread
and eat it, for this bread is My Body.
It shall be given up for you, and it
shall become our new covenant. And now
take this cup of wine, the blood of this new
covenant: it shall be shed, I promise,
for you. Remember and do this again for Me.
Everyone is drinking,

and as Judas
slips away into the destined night,

the meal done, the fourth toast offered, the group
begins cleanup: unsaddles the tables,
stacks the benches, extinguishes the lights.

Afterwards, the Man also slips away.

The Sorrowful Mysteries

I. Suffering in the Garden

Hematidrosis, a word precise and odd
is modern medicine's explanation
of a rare suffering, intense and hard,
in which sweat turns copiously crimson.
The patient, burdened by knowledge acursed,
sweating feverishly, feels so felled by dread
that the heart darts and capillaries burst
and blood punctures skin making the sweat red.
And the Man, bowed with the anxiety
that all human sin is redeemed through Him
when He is to suffer impiety,
humiliation and sadistic whim,
does sweat blood and wishes entirely
to shun this sacrifice of life and limb.

To shun this sacrifice of life and limb
the Man prays, and visions of the world's sins
play within His mind while His sight grows dim;
but against that wretchedness now begins
a weak strength that seeks appropriate words
to voice a truer sense of His mission.
He stops to take note of a sound of birds,
but it is no bird to which He'll listen.
An angel! When He opens up his eyes,
before Him stands a heavenly servant
bringing Him new strength that lets Him devise
a thought to embrace his predicament:

If this cup may not be taken away,
then Your will, Father, I gladly obey.

II. Scourging at the Pillar

Then Your will, Father, I gladly obey
whilst the gleeful Roman militia peels
the woolen mantle, gaily strips away
the tunic, jeeringly drags to His heels
the loincloth of modesty. Undressed
and humbled, He stands in silence while flocks
of onlookers cheer at a soldier's zest
for spitting on Him with curses and mocks.
They tie His wrists with moistened leather strings
and stretch His arms to the pillar's high clasp.
And one centurion's whip joyfully stings
the air in practice and makes the mob gasp.
His long hair and beard are matted with sweat
but fear now welcomes the proximate threat.

But fear now welcomes the proximate threat
of leathern lashes lacerating skin,
for now He accepts and will not regret
the torment where His triumph must begin.
And historians agree that the whips
were perfect tools to inflict a perfect woe,
made of leather with thongs of two thin strips
which each held the sharpened bone of an ewe.
The whips hum as they slash His naked back;
the lashes chant as they slice through His flesh;
the crops sing as the bones flay His ribs and back;
the leather croons as blood flies from His flesh.
His legs, His thighs, His neck, His burning cheeks—
Of blood and piss and shit this live-corpse reeks.

III. Crowning with Thorns

Of blood and piss and shit this live-corpse reeks.
But sixty lashes are never enough
to satisfy the horror-struck crowd that peeks
curious through fingers and mumbles gruff
encouragement. Soldiers search with irony
and find a consul's wine-shade robe, debris
of thorny brush, which experts of botany
suppose to be from the native lote-tree
(spinazizyphus) and dress Him as king
in royal-colored mantle, and the thorns,
now shaped to a pileum, are a ring
upon His head that proclaims and adorns:
The blood that oozes beneath those sharp spikes
is His blood whom Caesar ruthlessly strikes.

IV. Carrying of the Cross

Is His blood whom Caesar ruthlessly strikes
the blood of a man self-condemned to death
and Pilate and Caesar merely the sikes
that flow shortly, then lose their depth and breadth?
Yes. And the Roman way of punishment,
is more vicious, historians agree,
than any other practice of chastisement
known in ancient or modern savagery.
The patibulum, these experts define,
is the pole's crossbeam that creates the T,
heavy, thick and square, probably made of pine,
hauled by the scourged to the last agony.
These Roman tortures, so brutal, so slow:
These expressive symbols of earthly woe!

These expressive symbols of earthly woe
turn all-inclusive when He bears the beam
near Jerusalem's women of sorrow
and gives a warning final and extreme:
Not for Me, but for yourselves should you wail
Then Veronica, before he moves on,
wipes His sweaty, bloody brow with a veil
that retains His face as if it were drawn.
He steps forward so weakened and pale
that the guards enlist Simon Cyrenee
fearing His body, so emptied, so frail,
might not reach Pilate's promised misery.
Simon the unwilling assumes the bale;
The Man and he arrive at Calvary.

V. Nailing to the Cross

The Man and he arrive at "Calvary,"
or "Golgotha"—"the Skull's Place"—in Hebrew
and two rascals for acts of thievery
worth less harshness, perhaps, as their due.
Scoundrels deserve not this, but less so He
who lies between them on the sluttish ground
as if crimes could be love and honesty,
and who, like them, will have His arms re-bound
but only so that when nails drive through wrists,
He won't recoil, but merely writhe and shake
with undreamed of pain a soldier insists
lets Him die sooner, but fully awake.
Then the soldiers sign His patibulum
"King of the Jews." They laugh at His kingdom.

"King of the Jews," they laugh at His kingdom
as they elevate Him to His throne—
the laughter that resounds at martyrdom!
And He, broken now, knows Himself alone.
O Father, why have You forsaken me?
He speaks while His feet to the pole are tied
so that the soles touch the rough carpentry.
Then the pointed rust-iron nail is plied
impinging on flesh with each hammered thump,
breaking skin, cracking through the other side,
gashing wood, pinning His leg to the stump.
One foot pinned, the soldiers nail the next now:
"O King Without Kingdom!" they laugh and bow.

"O King Without Kingdom," they laugh and bow.
Might a king have ever been more bereft?
Physically broken from instep to brow
and from His cowardly followers cleft,
forsaken, alone, unwilling to seethe
with anger, He must push upon His feet,
pull up His arms and raise His chest to breathe,
but the effort is too hard to repeat
again and again: *It's done.* He lets knees
buckle and arms sag to full extention.
His belly concave; ribs, planks mid gullies:
Death on the rood is by suffocation.
This final giving in is the true icon of loss—
Defeated, disheartened, deserted, then dead: the Man on the
Cross.

As Mary sees the gibes, the whaling, the thorns,
the bitter walk toward death, the nails—she mourns.
But the long pilum forced into His chest
pierces her cracked heart, as Simeon expressed,
and pain—a mom's anguish, a disciple's grief—
infuses her body, knows no relief
except in the joyous signs she has seen
and in the words He spoke and what they mean.
She recalls them now and knows not to accept
this death, but knows not what more to expect.
This spear seems so final, the last concept
in a long humiliation unchecked
by any human sympathy, except
He embraced it knowing what would be wreaked.

The Glorious Mysteries

I. The Resurrection

Defeated, disheartened, deserted, then dead, the Man on the
Cross
is taken and cleaned and shrouded in linen and placed in a
tomb,
unused and virginal as, at His conception, was His mother's
womb.

His followers are afeared and scattered, completely at a loss,
but find themselves gravitating to the upper room
where, with the windows shuttered, they sit and do not talk in
the dark and gloom.

Dawns rise, nights pass; then joy cometh in the mourning after
the Sabbath:

When the rock rolls back, earth-quake loud,
the Roman soldiers quickly flee
leaving no witness there to see
the rising Lord shedding His shroud.

II. The Ascension

The son of a carpenter was killed
who died on a cross of woes
and taken to a tomb was filled
and wearing a dead man clothes.

Then came in the morn the sabbath day
The women who dressed Him so
and found from the tomb Him gone away.
"Now where, O where'd He go?"

In haste to Peter and the men they run
and give their story up.
The news of the empty tomb now done,
they all sit down to sup.

The Man of the cross appears to them
and speaks of His visit to Hell
and tells of the new Jerusalem
and there with them does dwell.

For forty days, for forty nights
He stayed and ate and prayed
and always moved within their sights
and made them less afraid.

Then comes the required time of change,
He has to bid them adieu
and takes them high on a mountain range
Always I will be with you.

They watch Him elevate and rise
and rise up like the dawn.
His glow, His clothes, they blind their eyes:
"O Where, O Where's the Lord gone?"

"He's gone to theFather in Heaven,"
a voice within them cries
"No longer to be with us even,
"No longer to say good-byes."

To their room they go, but saddened again
because emptiness again seems most;
then suddenly are they gladdened again
by fires of the Holy Ghost.

III. The Pentecost

♫♫ Come Holy Ghost, Creator blest,
and in our hearts take up thy rest. ♫♫

Before the Lord died and rose
Before the miracles of wine and bread
Before Isaiah called Him Immanuel
Yahweh renewed the covenant with Elijah.
Before the Lord died and rose
Before the miracle that cleaned the lepers
Before Elijah renewed the covenant
Yahweh gave Moses the Law.
Before the Lord died and rose
Before the miracle of the stilled storm
Before Moses received the Law
Yahweh made covenant with Abram
and Abraham offered His son,
but an angel stayed his hand.

The Feast of Weeks celebrates the harvest and the Law
Fifty days did Moses travel to Sinai
Fifty days from Unleavened Bread to the leavened bread,
first fruits of the harvest
and now
Fifty days from the Rising,
first fruits of the harvest:
the Spirit come upon them in the Upper Room
No mountain. No lightening. No immense storm. No
earthquake—
As if the Lord is done with drama,

Wants to tone down the threatricals.
Simple men, earthy women
cooks, epileptics, fishermen, merchants
taxcollectors, students, seamstresses, whores—
They are there, and there is here
and the Spirit come upon them in fire.
Small flames are quiet tongues, burning nothing
like Moses' bush, burning nothing
like Isaiah's lips, burning nothing
like Abraham's son.
For now the cooks
Are Moses, the epileptics
Are Elijah. Isaiah is a tentmaker.
The flame has made heroes of all.

After the Lord died and rose,
After the miracle of the fish and loaves
The Lord Immanuel—*God is with us*—leaves them
But the Spirit come upon them and stay

IV. The Assumption

Some say, "She died.
If the Lord had to die,
Could any alibi
to her betide?"
"She stayed alive
He rose, uncaged the crowd
of death, and that allowed
her to survive"—
others suppose.
But opposites agree
that the real mystery
is that she rose
to Heaven high—
that is, to God' presence
and His magnificence—
from earth to sky.
Soon it was done:
She rose aglow with light,
her hair and hands as bright,
a woman clothed with the sun.

V. The Coronation

♫♫ Salve, Salve, Salve, Regina! ♫♫

Heaven's crowned queen is a carpenter's wife.
Though she becomes the mother of a child,
she stays a true virgin all of her life.
She is God's chosen daughter, meek and mild,
and God's own mother the very same while.
These impossibles are unnatural shocks:
This woman is God's earthly paradox.

This woman is God's earthy paradox.
In that regard, she resembles her Son:
a King of kings who ministers to flocks,
three separate Godheads, but really just One,
God-With-Us even after His Ascension.
They restore the joy Eve and Adam fled:
He slays death; she crushes the serpent's head.

He slays death; she crushes the serpent's head.
She becomes the new mother, the new Eve:
through her bountiful breasts are nations fed—
all gifts, all graces, even when we grieve,
are given through her for us to receive,
for she is humanity's advocate, heaven and earth's go-between,
Mary, Mother, Daughter, Disciple, and Heaven's Crowned
Queen.

♫♫ Salve, Salve, Salve, Regina! ♫♫

Would you like to see your manuscript become a book?

If you are interested in becoming a PublishAmerica author, please submit your manuscript for possible publication to us at:

acquisitions@publishamerica.com

You may also mail in your manuscript to:

**PublishAmerica
PO Box 151
Frederick, MD 21705**

We also offer free graphics for Children's Picture Books!

---

www.publishamerica.com

CPSIA information can be obtained at www.ICGtesting.com
Printed in the USA
LVOW101252061012

301604LV00005B/16/P